CAMPBELL MORRIS

Fold Your Own Dinosaurs!

Important Notice

The dinosaurs in this book are sometimes rather complicated to make. It is really very important to first practise all the basic steps until you feel confident about them before starting on the beasts themselves.

Try all the base steps — the reverse folds, rabbit ear fold and especially the bird base — several times before starting. Your dinosaurs will thank you for it.

DIAGRAM ILLUSTRATION BY PAUL JACKSON

A PERIGEE BOOK

*In loving memory of Louise Lennon,
who gave constant support and encouragement
in all my literary endeavours,
no matter how trivial I felt they were.*

*Perigee Books
are published by
The Putnam Publishing Group
200 Madison Avenue
New York, NY 10016*

*First Perigee Edition 1993
First published in Australia by Angus & Robertson in 1988
This edition published by arrangement with Angus & Robertson
A division of HarperCollinsPublishers (Australia) Pty Ltd
25 Ryce Road, Pymble NSW 2073, Australia*

Library of Congress Cataloging-in-Publication Data

*Morris, Campbell, date.
    Fold your own dinosaurs / Campbell Morris ; diagram illustration
by Paul Jackson. — 1st Perigee ed.
        p.   cm.
    Summary: Provides instructions for folding paper to make twelve
realistic origami dinosaurs, including the stegosaurus,
tyrannosaurus, and triceratops.
    ISBN 0-399-51794-4 (alk. paper)
    1. Origami—Juvenile literature.   2. Dinosaurs in art—Juvenile
literature.   [1. Dinosaurs in art.   2. Origami.   3. Handicraft.]
I. Jackson, Paul, date.   ill.   II. Title.
TT870.M67   1993   92-32894   CIP   AC
736'.982—dc20*

*Cover design by Lisa Amoroso
Cover photo © by Jim McGuire*

*Printed in the United States of America
            6   7   8   9   10*

This book is printed on acid-free paper.

Family Togetherness through Dinosaurs

This book is designed initially for parent/child or family activity. A parent's or an older child's help and guidance will at first be needed by younger children on many of the models presented but, after a period of helpful togetherness and with lots of practise, children will be able to manage on their own.

An important start for all dinosaur makers is to take careful note of the folding symbols and to practise the basic steps until they are mastered before starting on the models themselves. The reverse folds, for example, may look complex but suddenly you'll find the knack, and you'll find it an extremely useful knack as you work your way through the prehistoric zoo!

Most models in this book begin with a square piece of paper and an easy method of making a square is shown on page 4.

Practise on plain sheets of paper to begin with. Make sure your paper is crisp, not flimsy. When you become proficient, you might like to try coloured paper. Many stationers or newsagents have coloured paper already cut square. Some types of paper even feature colour on one side and white on the other. This can add contrast to your dinosaurs.

Finally, be patient. . .and try not to fill your wastepaper basket full of crumpled paper too soon!

About Dinosaurs

These creatures have fascinated people for hundreds of years but no one knew much about them until recently. It is interesting to note the mystery behind their disappearance from the face of the earth. Many reasons for this have been suggested, which include a change in climate, a change in vegetation and large-scale meteorite destruction. Perhaps most importantly, we should find out how dinosaurs came to be and what impact they have had on the world today.

Dinosaurs are often seen as being the complete array of prehistoric creatures that once inhabited our planet. Dinosaurs were in fact a distinct group of reptiles. They were characterised by a fully supportive limb structure — meaning that the limbs supported the body from underneath, raising the body off the ground. Other prehistoric creatures did not fully utilise their limbs to support the body. They rested their bellies on the ground and propelled themselves forward by pushing with the tail and swinging the trunk. Dinosaurs also walked using their toes rather than just the soles of their feet. Biped dinosaurs could run on their hind legs alone, not depending on all four legs.

New theories suggest that mammals and birds such as the emu are descendants of dinosaurs. Scientists are uncovering new evidence that suggests that dinosaurs were not just cumbersome creatures that lumbered around swampland but agile land dwellers.

The dinosaurs and other prehistoric beasts presented in this book did not all exist at the same time. The Stegosaurus, Archaeopteryx and Brontosaurus, for instance, all existed during the late Jurassic period some 145 million years ago. The Tyrannosaurus, Triceratops and Corythosaurus existed during the late Cretaceous period around eighty million years ago.

I suggest you investigate your library to find out more about these fascinating creatures. In the meantime, you can learn to make your own dinosaurs with a minimum of fuss. Happy folding!

Folding Techniques

Symbols and Procedures

Basic symbols and procedures have been included at the bottom of each project.

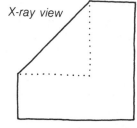 X-ray view

 hold here

pull

push here

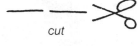
cut

turn over

fold to the front

fold behind

unfold

fold and unfold

fold one dot onto the other

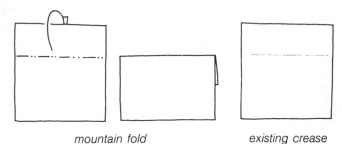

valley fold

mountain fold

existing crease

How to Make a Square

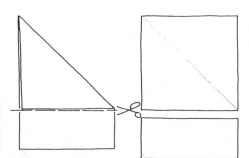

4

1

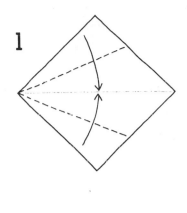

2

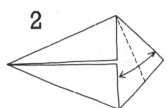

3

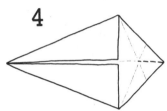

4

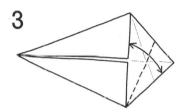

How to Make a Rabbit Ear Fold

This is a very useful folding procedure to have tucked away in your brain. The rabbit ear fold enables the origamist to create more points to work with. One can fold ears, add legs and so on. Here's how it's done:

1
Using a small square of paper fold in the sides to the centre.
2
Valley fold and unfold.
3
Valley fold the opposite side and unfold.
4
Valley fold the corner to the centre of the creases to make a point — the rabbit ear.
5
Fold or push the model in along crease lines.
6
Almost there.
7
It's complete.

5

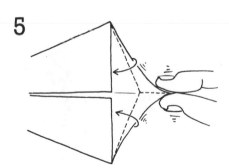

6

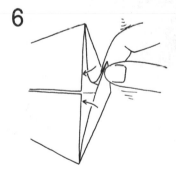

7

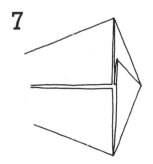

This is what the symbol for a rabbit ear fold looks like.

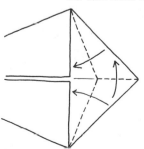

How to Make an Inside Reverse Fold

Some of the smaller folds such as those that make heads and feet require patience. By practising with small pieces of paper you can gain experience in making the perfect dinosaur — to the finest detail.

1
Fold a paper square in half diagonally then unfold. It should look like this with a crease down the centre. Fold the two sides in towards the centre.

2
Fold the model in half.

3
Fold the top corner towards you along the line.

4
Crease and unfold.

5
Fold the top corner away from you along the same line.

6
Crease and unfold.

7
The model is now creased ready for the inside reverse fold.

8
Open the model at the top, push the peak down.

9
The centre of the peak folds inwards.

10
Almost there.

11
A completed inside reverse fold.

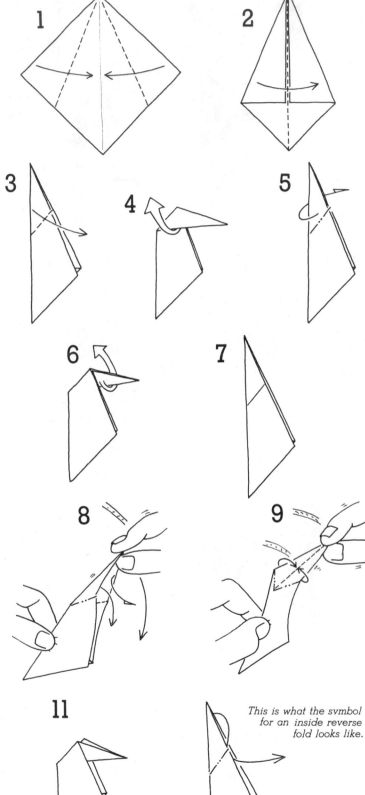

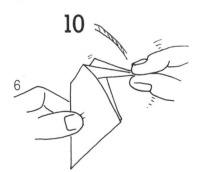

This is what the symbol for an inside reverse fold looks like.

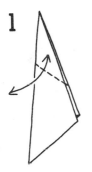

1

2

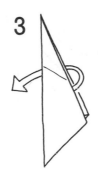

3

How to Make an Outside Reverse Fold

Another common folding procedure often used to make heads and feet. Start with steps 1 and 2 of the inside reverse fold.

1
Fold towards you and unfold.

2
Fold away from you and unfold.

3
Open out the model.

4
Push in at this point.

5
Pull the top corner outwards.

6
The model from the other side — while pulling back the top, bring the bottom two corners together.

7a & b
Two views of the completed model.

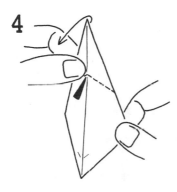

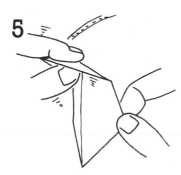

4

5

6

This is what the symbol for an outside reverse fold looks like.

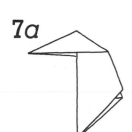

7a

7b

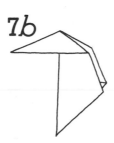

How to Make
The Bird Base

This is perhaps the most widely used basic fold in origami. The "Flapping Bird" is a famous derivative, and countless numbers of birds and beasts have been created from the bird base. You will not find a "flapping dinosaur" in this book; however, many of these dinosaur designs utilise the bird base.

1
Begin with a square piece of paper and fold it in half from corner to corner and unfold.

2
Fold in half again as shown, and unfold.

3
Turn the paper over.

4
The valley folds are now mountain folds!

5
Fold and unfold.

6
Fold the model in half.

7
Holding the sides together push the corners into the centre.

8
Flatten the model.

9
Fold the front flaps into the centre crease.

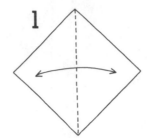

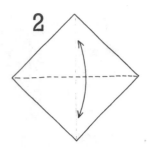

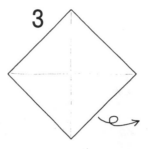

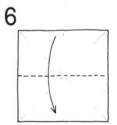

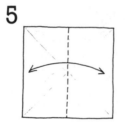

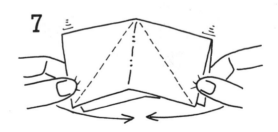

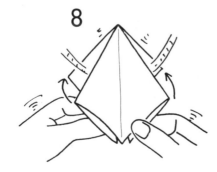

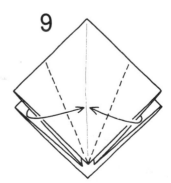

10

11

12

13

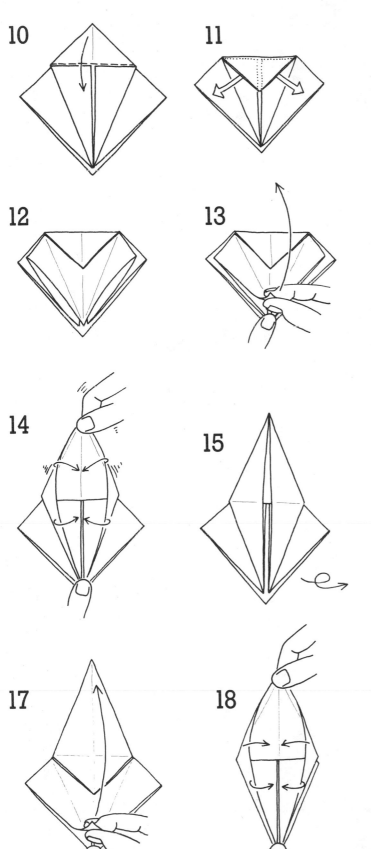

15

16

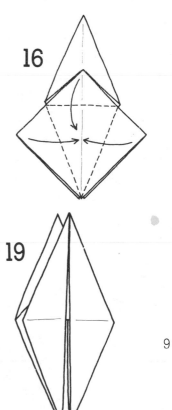

17

18

19

10
Fold the top corner in.
11
Unfold both side flaps.
12
Your model now looks like this.
13
With one hand hold all but the top flap and with the other hand fold back the top flap.
14
The sides will automatically start to fold in.
15
Press them firmly in place and turn the model over.
16
Repeat steps 9 to 13 as before.
17
Fold the top flap up as shown.
18
Press the sides into the centre.
19
The completed bird base.

9

Plesiosaurus

Although not a true dinosaur, the Plesiosaurus was one of the earliest reptiles living in the sea. Its average length was around four metres (thirteen feet) — a bit large for your fish tank, though a paper model would fit nicely!

1
Use an 8½" square piece of paper. Having creased it in half diagonally, fold the sides in as shown.

2
Fold the top flaps back as shown.

3
Turn the model over.

4
Fold the sides in towards the centre as shown.

5
Open out the top flaps.

6
Crease the top flaps where shown.

7
Then form a rabbit ear on each side.

8
Fold where indicated.

9
Unfold.

10

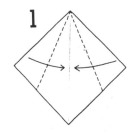
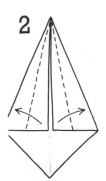
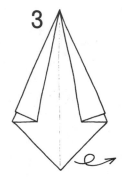
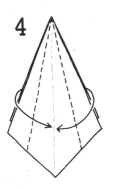

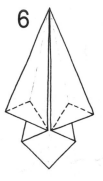
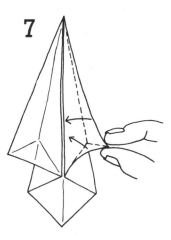

 fold and unfold

fold one dot onto the other

cut

 turn over

fold to the front

 fold behind

O hold here

 pull

 push here

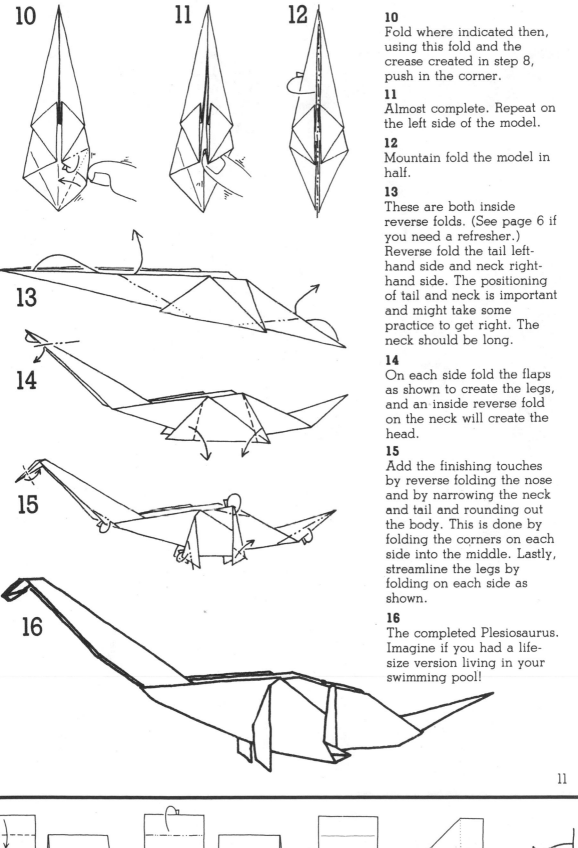

10
Fold where indicated then, using this fold and the crease created in step 8, push in the corner.

11
Almost complete. Repeat on the left side of the model.

12
Mountain fold the model in half.

13
These are both inside reverse folds. (See page 6 if you need a refresher.) Reverse fold the tail left-hand side and neck right-hand side. The positioning of tail and neck is important and might take some practice to get right. The neck should be long.

14
On each side fold the flaps as shown to create the legs, and an inside reverse fold on the neck will create the head.

15
Add the finishing touches by reverse folding the nose and by narrowing the neck and tail and rounding out the body. This is done by folding the corners on each side into the middle. Lastly, streamline the legs by folding on each side as shown.

16
The completed Plesiosaurus. Imagine if you had a life-size version living in your swimming pool!

valley fold   *mountain fold*   *existing crease*   *X-ray view*   *unfold*

Pterodactyl

While the Pterodactyl is not classed as a true dinosaur, this is what I call "building the perfect beast". Not only does this model look like the primitive flying creature but it actually flies too! A well-folded Pterodactyl can grace any bird cage.

1
Begin with a rectangular sheet of paper (8½" × 11"). Make a centre crease by folding it in half widthwise, then fold the corner in as shown.

2
Fold the flap back along the centre crease.

3
Fold along line to bring two spots together.

4
Fold the overlapping flap back along the centre crease.

5
In preparation for making rabbit ears fold along each of the dashes as shown, then unfold.

6
Pinch in the edges to form a rabbit ear on each side.

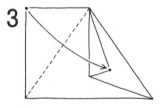

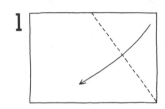

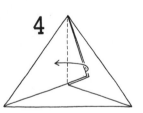

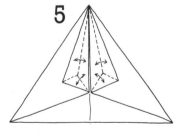

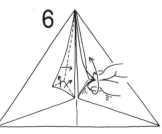

 fold and unfold

 fold one dot onto the other

cut

 turn over

 fold to the front

 fold behind

 hold here

 pull

push here

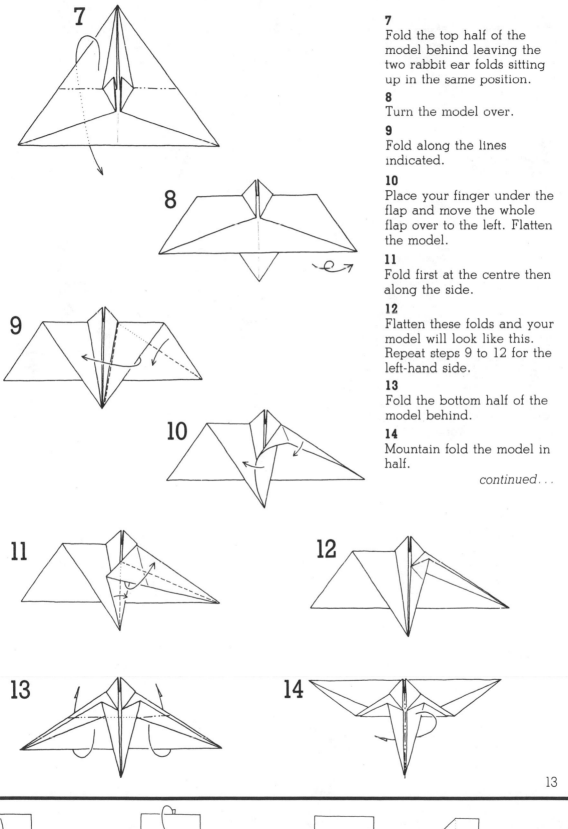

7
Fold the top half of the model behind leaving the two rabbit ear folds sitting up in the same position.

8
Turn the model over.

9
Fold along the lines indicated.

10
Place your finger under the flap and move the whole flap over to the left. Flatten the model.

11
Fold first at the centre then along the side.

12
Flatten these folds and your model will look like this. Repeat steps 9 to 12 for the left-hand side.

13
Fold the bottom half of the model behind.

14
Mountain fold the model in half.

continued...

13

valley fold   *mountain fold*   *existing crease*   *X-ray view*   *unfold*

15
Reverse fold the neck.

16
Open out the neck section and fold back on each side where indicated.

17
Fold the wings down.

18
Gently curve the wings upwards.

19
Fold the head section as shown, using a reverse fold.

20
Now open out the nose and use a mountain fold to swing the beak forward.

21
The head section complete.

22
The completed Pterodactyl. Throw gently away from you towards the nearest cat, guinea pig etc., and watch it swoop in for the kill! Try folding larger versions using coloured paper.

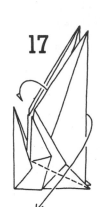

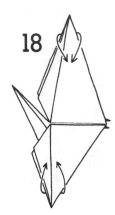

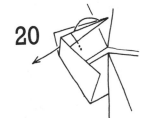

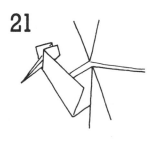

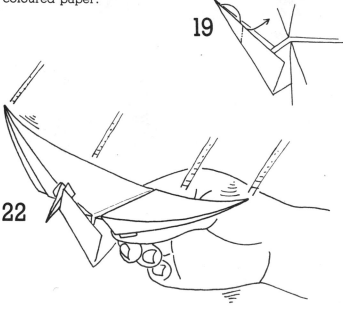

⟵⟶ *fold and unfold*	⟲➚ *turn over*	O *hold here*
•⌒• *fold one dot onto the other*	⟶ *fold to the front*	*pull*
– – ✂ *cut*	⟶ *fold behind*	▶ *push here*

Dimetrodon

This amazing creature, although not a true dinosaur, would lumber along on all fours, occasionally resting on its belly to observe its surroundings. Although the Dimetrodon is a cold-blooded reptile, scientists have determined that the creature's fin acted as some type of heat exchanger. The fin would trap heat and raise the temperature of the body. It's such a pity these creatures do not exist today. Their fins could be cheaper to use than conventional air conditioners!

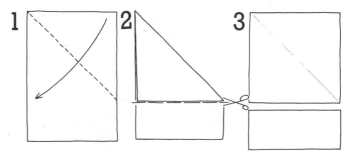

1, 2 & 3
From an 8½" × 11" sheet of paper make a square but do not discard the smaller piece of paper.

4
Make up to step 9 of the bird base. (See page 8.)

5
Open out one of the left-hand corners.

6
Flatten the flap so that the crease is centred.

7
Fold the corners to the middle crease as shown.

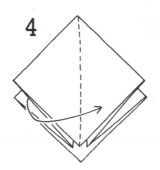

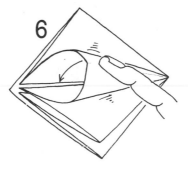

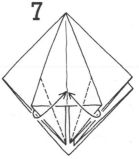

continued...

15

valle y fold

mountain fold

existing crease

X-ray view

unfold

8
Unfold.

9
Open out the corner and mountain fold as shown. This corner is to be tucked in...

10
...like this.

11
Repeat steps 9 and 10 on the left-hand side then swing the top right-hand flap up.

12
Flatten this fold as in step 6.

13
Repeat steps 7 to 11 then swing the top left-hand flap across.

14
Your model will look like this. Turn it over.

15
Fold where shown and unfold. Now swing the top layer upwards while holding the layers beneath. (Similar to steps 9 to 14 of the bird base on pages 8 and 9.)

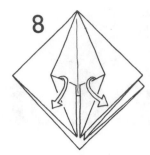

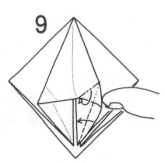

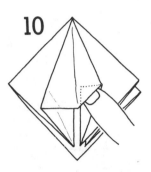

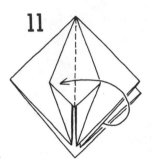

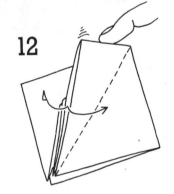

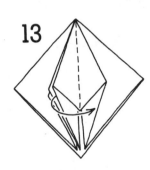

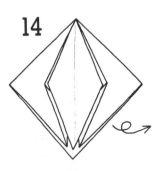

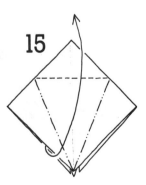

 fold and unfold

 fold one dot onto the other

 cut

 turn over

fold to the front

fold behind

○ hold here

 pull

► push here

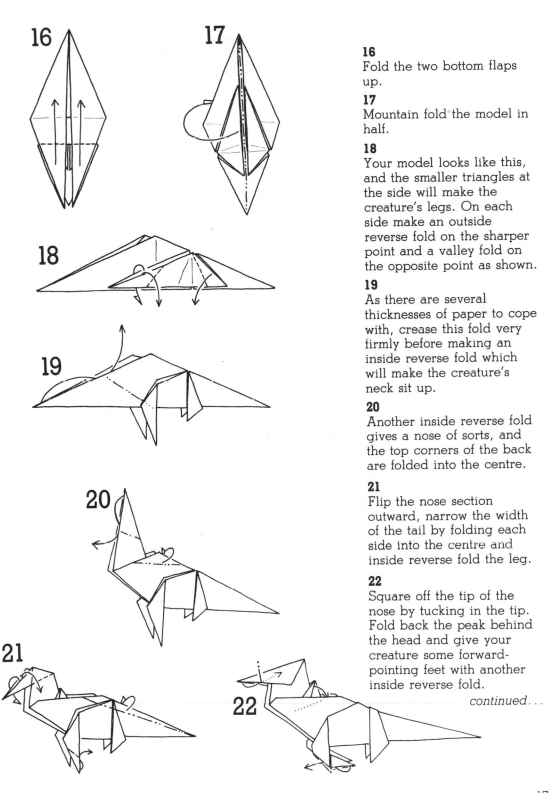

16
Fold the two bottom flaps up.

17
Mountain fold the model in half.

18
Your model looks like this, and the smaller triangles at the side will make the creature's legs. On each side make an outside reverse fold on the sharper point and a valley fold on the opposite point as shown.

19
As there are several thicknesses of paper to cope with, crease this fold very firmly before making an inside reverse fold which will make the creature's neck sit up.

20
Another inside reverse fold gives a nose of sorts, and the top corners of the back are folded into the centre.

21
Flip the nose section outward, narrow the width of the tail by folding each side into the centre and inside reverse fold the leg.

22
Square off the tip of the nose by tucking in the tip. Fold back the peak behind the head and give your creature some forward-pointing feet with another inside reverse fold.

continued . . .

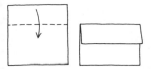

valley fold

mountain fold

existing crease

X-ray view

unfold

Fin Section

23
With a compass draw and cut out a semi-circle using about two-thirds of the length of the off-cut paper.

24
Using mountain and valley folds, fold this back and forth to make the fan-like fin.

25
Glue the bottom section of the fin and slot it into the centre of the body.

26
Your finished Dimetrodon will be your greatest fan!

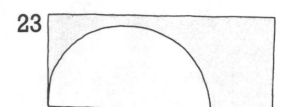

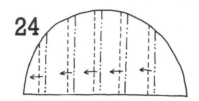

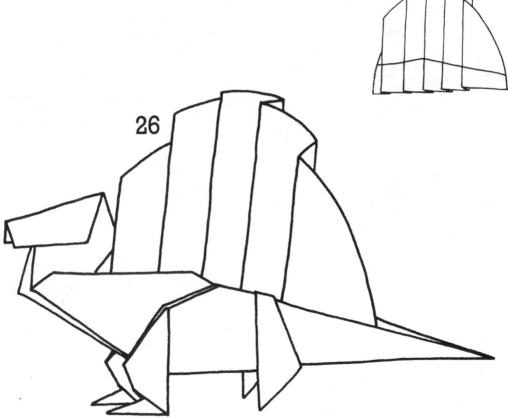

 fold and unfold

 fold one dot onto the other

 cut

 turn over

fold to the front

fold behind

○ hold here

 pull

 push here

Massospondylus

This creature lived during the late Triassic/early Jurassic time approximately 190 million years ago and belongs to the prosauropod group of dinosaurs. They were generally small — even as small as two metres (six-and-a-half feet). It has been suggested by scientists that the creature was partly biped. Most of the time, however, it would move around on all fours; that's something to ponder on!

1
Make up to step 16 of Dimetrodon (pages 15, 16 and 17) and fold the left-hand flap over to the right-hand side.

2
Fold to join the dots.

3
Fold the top right flap to the left.

4
Fold the remaining right flap to the left.

5
Fold to join the dots.

6
Swing the flap back to the right.

continued...

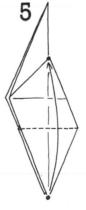

valley fold

mountain fold

existing crease

X-ray view

unfold

7
On each side fold inwards bringing dot to dot.

8
On each side crease well and make an inside reverse fold.

9
Fold the top triangle upward on each side...

10
...then unfold.

11
Fold the corners in towards the centre, crease and flatten.

12
Turn the model over.

13
Under the lower peak on each side you'll find a point to play with. Follow the arrows and inside reverse fold the points to make the front legs. The dots represent an inside reverse fold on the hidden flaps. Fold the bottom edges towards the centre joining dots to dots. The rear legs should automatically be revealed.

14
Mountain fold the model in half.

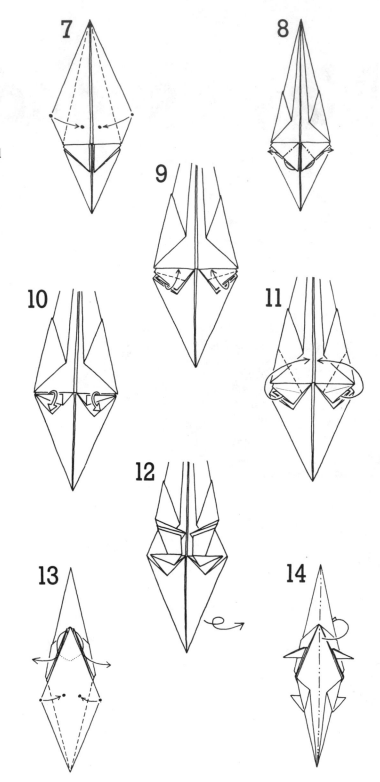

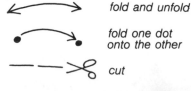 fold and unfold	 turn over	O hold here
fold one dot onto the other	fold to the front	pull
cut	fold behind	push here

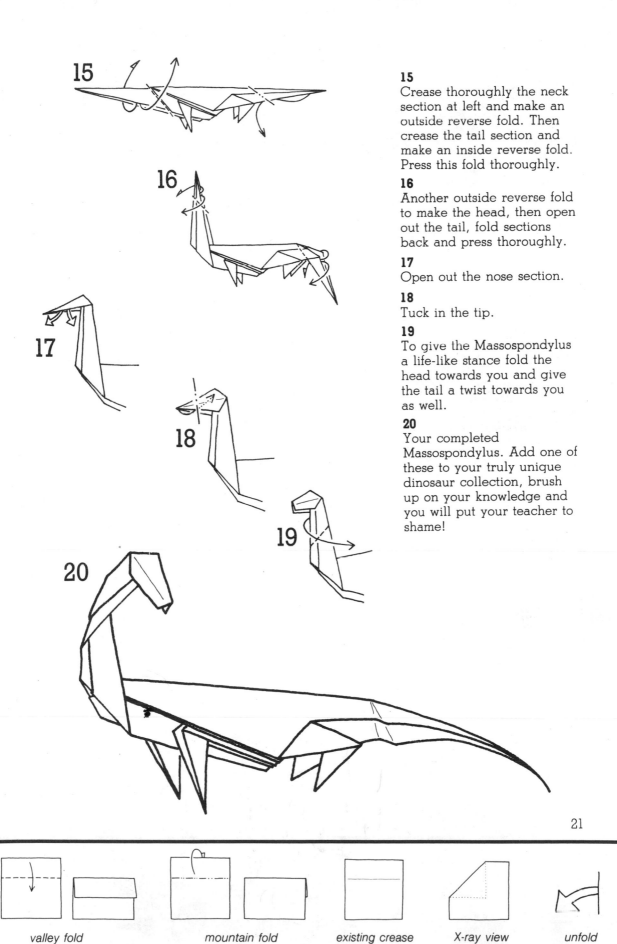

15
Crease thoroughly the neck section at left and make an outside reverse fold. Then crease the tail section and make an inside reverse fold. Press this fold thoroughly.

16
Another outside reverse fold to make the head, then open out the tail, fold sections back and press thoroughly.

17
Open out the nose section.

18
Tuck in the tip.

19
To give the Massospondylus a life-like stance fold the head towards you and give the tail a twist towards you as well.

20
Your completed Massospondylus. Add one of these to your truly unique dinosaur collection, brush up on your knowledge and you will put your teacher to shame!

valley fold   *mountain fold*   *existing crease*   *X-ray view*   *unfold*

Stegosaurus

This is a fascinating plated dinosaur that lived mainly in western North America more than 140 million years ago during the late Jurassic period. The Stegosaurus grew to more than six metres (twenty feet) in length. No one is quite sure what function the plates had. Some scientists suggest they acted as heat exchangers in the same way as the Dimetrodon's fin worked. Others argue that it is more likely that the plates evolved out of a need for the creature to defend itself.

The Stegosaurus was definitely a robust and heavy creature.

1, 2 & 3
From a rectangular sheet of paper (8½" × 11"), make an 8½" square; keep the off-cut strip.

4
Work steps 4 to 17 of the Dimetrodon (pages 15, 16 and 17), and inside reverse fold the neck section.

5
Another inside reverse fold to make the head section and one each side to start work on the front feet. The back feet simply need a valley fold on each side.

22

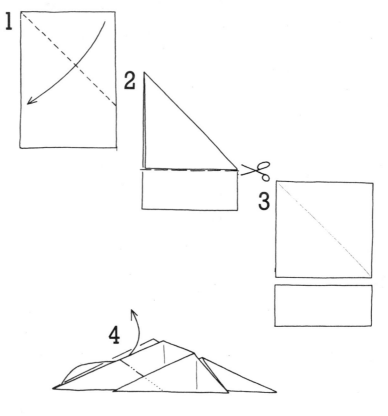

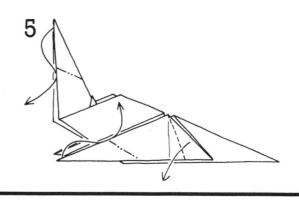

---

 fold and unfold

 fold one dot onto the other

 cut

 turn over

fold to the front

fold behind

○ hold here

 pull

▶ push here

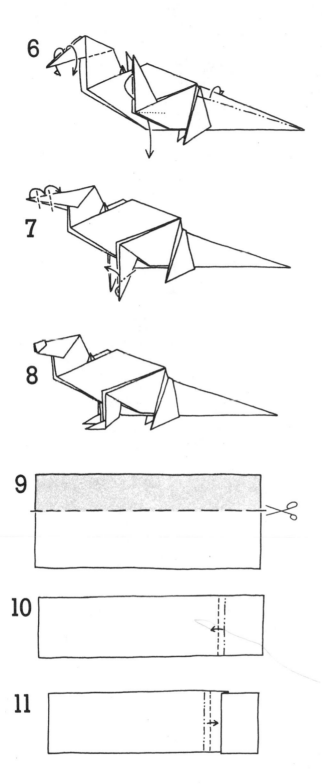

6
Open out the flaps of the head and press them out and down. On both sides open out the front feet, crease and make an inside reverse fold. Slim down the tail by folding each side into the centre.

7
Fold the nose back twice and reverse fold the front legs on each side to form the feet.

8
The creature without its armour.

Fan Arrangement
9
Remember that off-cut piece of paper which you kept? Cut it to 4 cm wide × 21 cm long (1½ in. × 8½ in.). Working with such small pieces of paper, this is the really fiddly bit which needs patience along with nimble fingers. Smaller children will find it simpler to cut out a fin shape. Or, if you have a fancy for something a lot more intricate, the fan can be made as follows:

10
About 4 cm (1½ in.) from the right-hand side begin by making a mountain and valley fold as indicated.

11
About 1 cm (½ in.) along, mountain fold and valley fold again bringing the fold towards the first one.

continued...

valley fold

mountain fold

existing crease

X-ray view

unfold

12
The whole strip is folded in this way allowing to make four fins, each fin about 1 cm (½ in.) in width. The Stegosaurus, of course, has more fins but folding would become complicated. You'll still love the results!

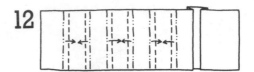

13
Crease along the smaller fold line first then fold the larger ones.

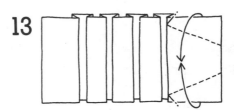

14
The fiddly small corners should then automatically turn back and will need flattening.

15
Crease the corners of the fins.

16
Uncrease.

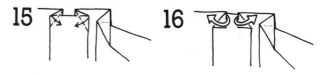

17
Push in these corners and flatten the fold.

18
Fold the small flap down.

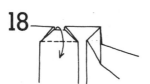

19
The completed fin tip. Repeat this on each fin tip top and bottom.

fold and unfold		 *turn over*		O *hold here*
fold one dot onto the other		→ *fold to the front*		*pull*
cut		*fold behind*		► *push here*

20

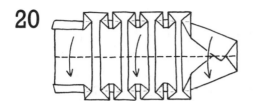

20
Fold in the left-hand edges as shown and valley fold the model in half.

21
With both hands place thumb and finger on each end of the fan arrangement and pull to make a curve.

22
Round out the fin points by folding each into the centre.

23
Glue the base of the fin as shown. You are now ready to slot the fan arrangement into the Stegosaurus body.

24
The completed Stegosaurus. Make a few for your dinosaur army!

21

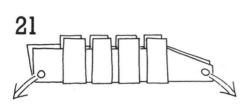

22

23

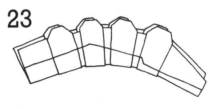

24

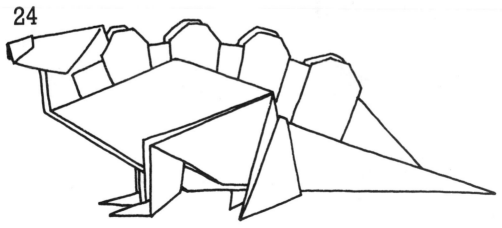

valley fold

mountain fold

existing crease

X-ray view

unfold

Brontosaurus

Perhaps because of its size this is one of the most recognisable dinosaurs. It was big — very big! The "thunder lizard" lumbered around our planet during the late Jurassic period, 140 million years ago. Its typical length was around twenty-two metres (seventy-two feet), and with a weight of over twenty-five tonnes (twenty-five tons) it could flatten any elephant! The Brontosaurus belongs to the sauropod group of dinosaurs which feature the classic dinosaur shape. These creatures were vegetarian so if you happen to entertain one today a tossed salad and some French dressing won't go astray.

1
Begin by making up to step 7 of the Massospondylus (pages 19 and 20). Turn the model over.

2
Inside reverse fold the two hidden flaps as shown. This will form the legs.

3
Fold the model in half.

4
Make an inside reverse fold

	fold and unfold	turn over
fold one dot onto the other		fold to the front
cut		fold behind

fold and unfold

fold one dot onto the other

cut

turn over

fold to the front

fold behind

hold here

pull

push here

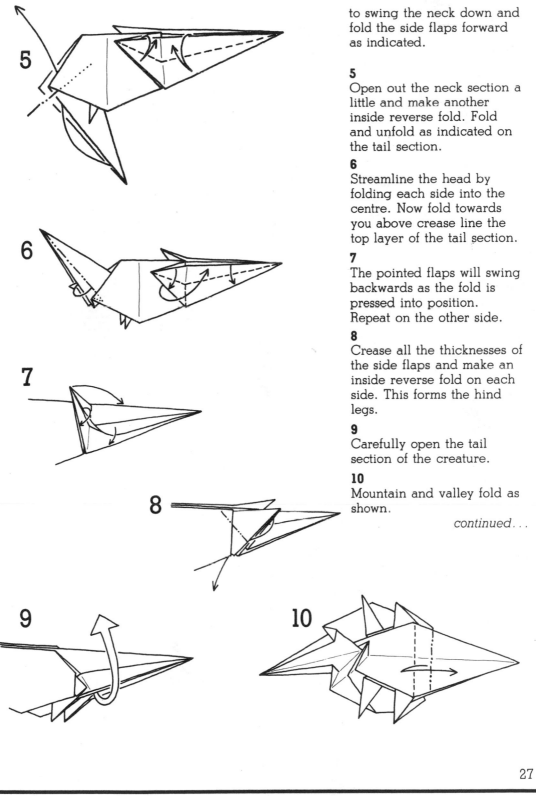

to swing the neck down and
fold the side flaps forward
as indicated.

5
Open out the neck section a
little and make another
inside reverse fold. Fold
and unfold as indicated on
the tail section.

6
Streamline the head by
folding each side into the
centre. Now fold towards
you above crease line the
top layer of the tail section.

7
The pointed flaps will swing
backwards as the fold is
pressed into position.
Repeat on the other side.

8
Crease all the thicknesses of
the side flaps and make an
inside reverse fold on each
side. This forms the hind
legs.

9
Carefully open the tail
section of the creature.

10
Mountain and valley fold as
shown.

continued...

valley fold

mountain fold

existing crease

X-ray view

unfold

11

Fold the model in half again.

12

Inside reverse fold the neck to make a head. By holding both points of the tail section pull the tail downwards.

13

Fold the creature's nose under, then open tail out slightly and push in the spine of the tail to make it narrow. Curl the body and tail. You could even curve the neck.

14

Your completed Brontosaurus...don't let it step on anyone!

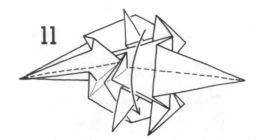

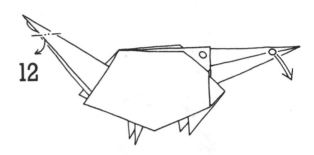

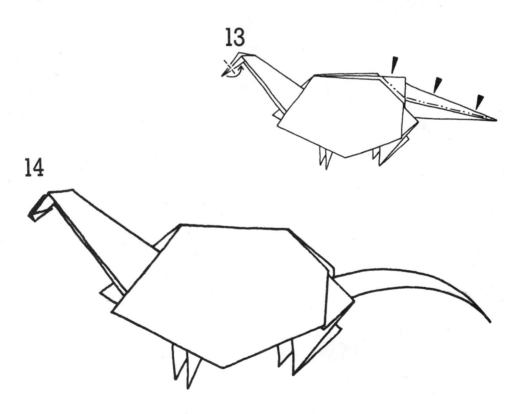

 fold and unfold

 fold one dot onto the other

 cut

turn over

fold to the front

fold behind

O   hold here

 pull

 push here

Tyrannosaurus

Now you can make this ferocious, meat-eating dinosaur in the comfort of your own home. But — a warning — don't let the Tyrannosaurus near your freezer!

1
Begin with the bird base (see pages 8 and 9), then fold the top flaps down.

2
Fold dot to dot where indicated, crease well and unfold.

3
Mountain fold in the same position, crease well and unfold.

4
Carefully open out the model.

5
The creases made in steps 2 and 3 will be clearly seen.

6
Push in the point as shown.

7
Nearly there.

continued...

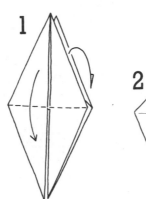

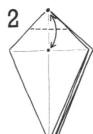

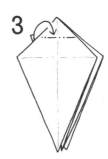

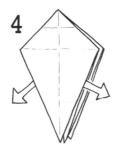

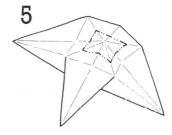

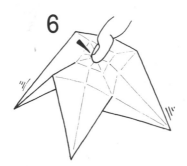

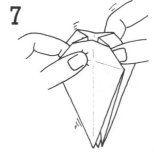

29

---

valley fold

mountain fold

existing crease

X-ray view

unfold

8
Swing the bottom flaps up on both sides.

9
Crease and make an inside reverse fold on both points.

10
This is the crease pattern for rabbit's ears. (See page 5 if you need a refresher.)

11
Pinch the sides together and the peak automatically comes forward. Press it to the left. Repeat the rabbit ear steps on the other side.

12
Fold back both rabbit ears as indicated. These will eventually become legs.

13
Crease and pull up the head section.

14
On each side fold down the leg sections.

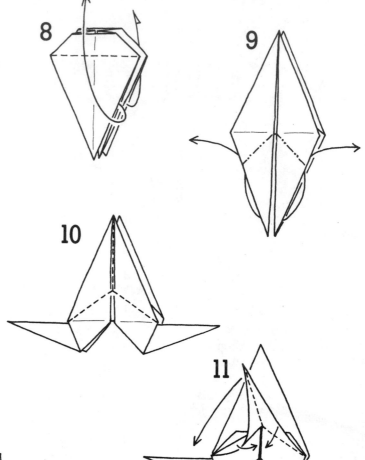

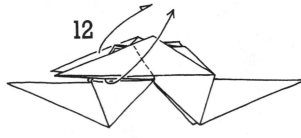

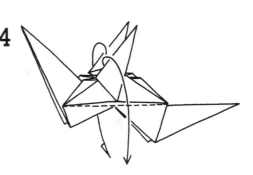

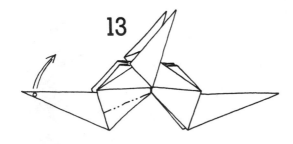

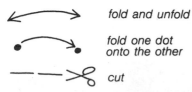 fold and unfold		turn over	O	hold here
fold one dot onto the other		fold to the front		pull
cut		fold behind		push here

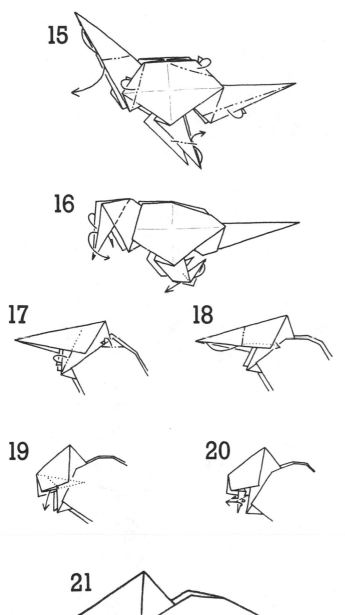

15

Crease and reverse fold the head. Fold the shoulder flaps on each side back inside the body. Fold the back corners inside to shape the body. Streamline the tail and inside reverse fold the feet.

16

Turn the head flaps outwards and press against the neck. Swing the feet forward with another inside reverse fold.

17

Shape under the head and shoulders by folding into the centre on each side. The first fold shapes the creature's small front legs.

18

Inside reverse fold the pointed nose section.

19

Inside reverse fold the tucked-in tip of the head.

20

Another inside reverse fold will create teeth. Trial and error will make it right.

21

The completed Tyrannosaurus.

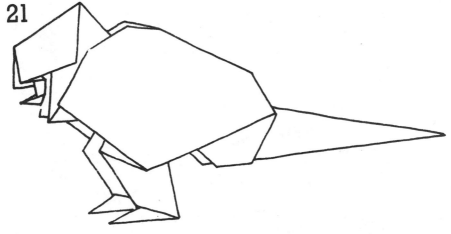

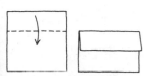

valley fold

mountain fold

existing crease

X-ray view

unfold

Tarbosaurus

Like the Tyrannosaurus, the
Tarbosaurus belonged to the
group of meat-eaters called
carnosaurs. There were
many species of carnosaurs
during the late Cretaceous
period about 100 million
years ago. I suggest you
delve further into the
mysteries of the dinosaurs at
your library — you never
know what new creatures
can be made from paper! If
you have made the
Tyrannosaurus this one will
be simple. Steps 1 to 13 are
the same and the teeth and
feet are also made in the
same way.

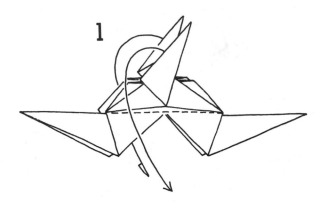

1
Using a bird base make up
to step 13 of the
Tyrannosaurus (pages 29
and 30). Swing the side
flaps down to form the legs.

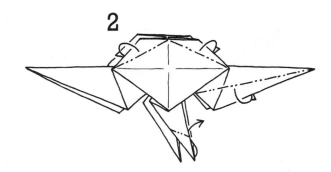

2
Streamline the body and the
tail on each side by folding
corners in to the middle.
Inside reverse fold the legs
to form feet.

3
Crease then outside reverse
fold the head. Crease and
inside reverse fold both the
feet and the tail.

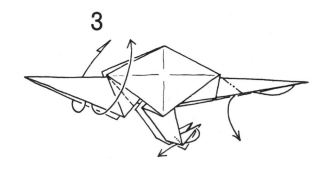

---

fold and unfold	↪ *turn over*	O *hold here*	
•⁀➤ *fold one dot onto the other*	→ *fold to the front*	*pull*	
cut	↳ *fold behind*	► *push here*	

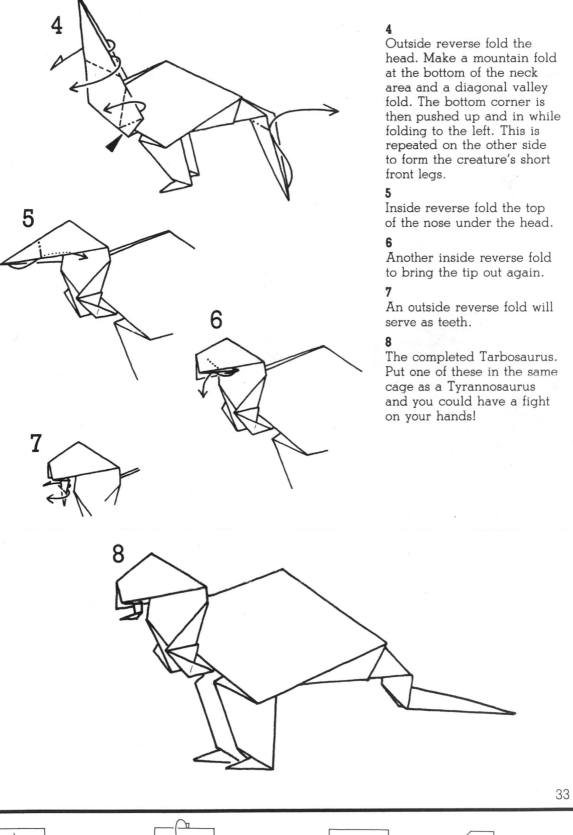

4

Outside reverse fold the head. Make a mountain fold at the bottom of the neck area and a diagonal valley fold. The bottom corner is then pushed up and in while folding to the left. This is repeated on the other side to form the creature's short front legs.

5

Inside reverse fold the top of the nose under the head.

6

Another inside reverse fold to bring the tip out again.

7

An outside reverse fold will serve as teeth.

8

The completed Tarbosaurus. Put one of these in the same cage as a Tyrannosaurus and you could have a fight on your hands!

valley fold

mountain fold

existing crease

X-ray view

unfold

Triceratops

This amazing rhinoceros-like dinosaur can now be folded out of paper in the comfort of your own home, classroom or during a boring lecture! The Triceratops belongs to the ceratopian group of dinosaurs which featured horns and armoured plating. Triceratops had three horns; other creatures of the same group may only have had one. They fed on vegetation and, unlike other dinosaurs, were good at self-defence against the Tyrannosaurus. The neck frill was solid and provided good protection.

1, 2 & 3

This model requires two pieces of paper... but the results are definitely worth it! Begin with a piece of rectangular paper (8½" × 11") or paper of the same proportion. Make a square, and use the off-cut to make a smaller square. This ensures the correct scaling of the two pieces.

4

Using the bird base make up to step 10 of the Tyrannosaurus (pages 29 and 30) and fold the top flaps down where indicated.

5

On each side fold back the bottom flaps...

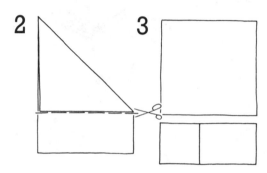

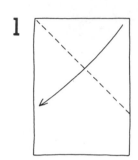

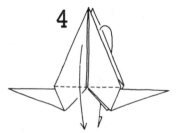

fold and unfold	turn over	O hold here
fold one dot onto the other	fold to the front	pull
cut	fold behind	push here

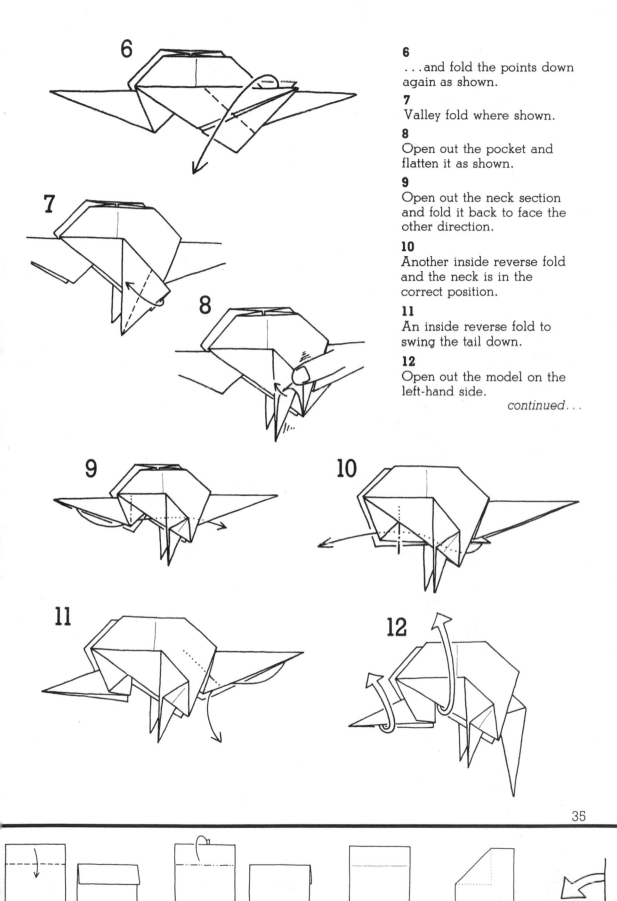

6
. . .and fold the points down
again as shown.

7
Valley fold where shown.

8
Open out the pocket and
flatten it as shown.

9
Open out the neck section
and fold it back to face the
other direction.

10
Another inside reverse fold
and the neck is in the
correct position.

11
An inside reverse fold to
swing the tail down.

12
Open out the model on the
left-hand side.

continued. . .

valley fold	*mountain fold*	*existing crease*	*X-ray view*	*unfold*

13

The left-hand point will form two of Triceratops's horns. Narrow this carefully as shown folding all in towards the middle and flattening the fold.

14

Nearly complete. Fold the model back in half.

15

Fold back the flaps on the left — this will become part of the neck frill armour and front legs. Round out the body by folding each corner into the centre, as shown. Inside reverse fold the tip of the tail and the legs to make feet.

16

Fold the left flaps back as shown and, to give the legs a bit of extra muscle, fold as shown. It's fiddly but looks good once you manage it. Pull neck up so that it is parallel to the underside of the belly.

17

Crease and outside reverse fold the horn section.

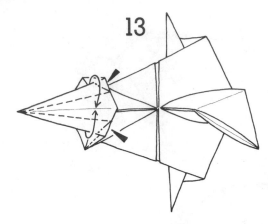

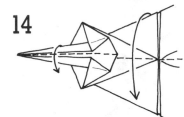

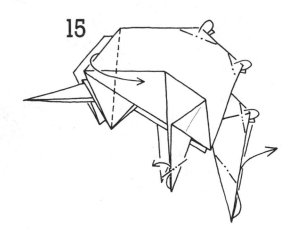

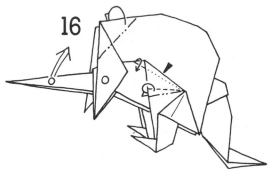

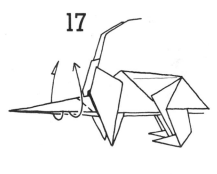

 fold and unfold

 fold one dot onto the other

 cut

 turn over

fold to the front

fold behind

O   hold here

 pull

▶   push here

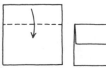

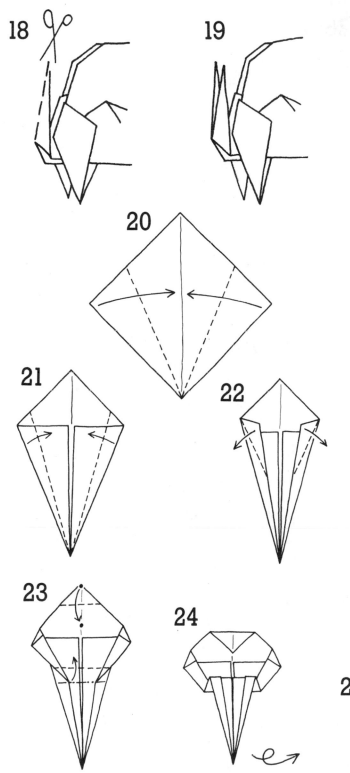

18

The dotted lines indicate a cut. Oh, yes...I'm sorry you have to use scissors but I insist the results will be more than worth it! Cut down the middle of the neck point to make two points which will become horns.

19

Having performed this task you can put the headless dinosaur to one side and begin on the head section.

Head Section

20

Remember that smaller piece of paper? If it hasn't been made into a paper plane, grab it, crease fold in half diagonally then open out and fold the edges in as shown.

21

Fold edges in to narrow the paper.

22

Fold points out as shown.

23

Mountain and valley fold in the middle as indicated and fold dot to dot at the top.

24

Turn the head over.

25

Fold the point with a valley fold, a mountain fold and another valley fold, and shape the top by tacking back corners as shown.

continued...

37

| valley fold | mountain fold | existing crease | X-ray view | unfold |

26
Fold the model in half.

27
Hold the base of the nose and pull the horn up.

28
Hold the nose section and pull the right side upwards.

29
Using a scalpel point or scissors point, bore a slit right through the head. Don't worry if it gives the creature a headache!

30
Fitting head section to the body section:
Let's hope the head fits the beast! Enlarge the slits if it doesn't. The two points on the neck section should slip comfortably through the two slits in the head. Slide them through to the base of the points.

31
The completed Triceratops — a worthwhile foe for any matador!

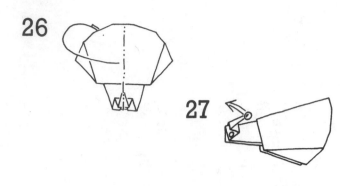

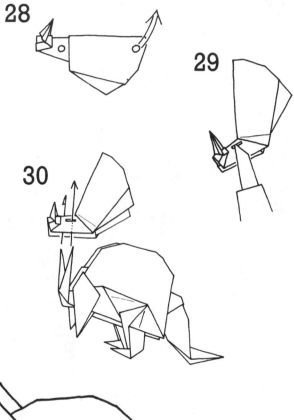

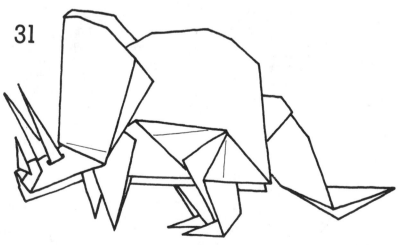

fold and unfold	turn over	⭕	hold here
• ⟶ • fold one dot onto the other	fold to the front		pull
— ✂ cut	fold behind	▶	push here

Archaeopteryx

Is it a dinosaur or is it a bird? Scientists have a theory that birds are descendants of the small nimble biped dinosaurs — namely coelurosaurian dinosaurs. The Archaeopteryx, meaning "ancient wing", lived as long ago as the Jurassic period — some 150 million years ago. It was a dinosaur that actually had feathers! The creature represents a true transition from dinosaur to bird and should probably be described as a primitive bird with reptilian features. How the creatures developed feathers and wings is unknown. Maybe the size of the smaller dinosaurs made them vulnerable to larger prey, so that they learned to climb trees, developed primitive wings and learned to glide.

1
Fold a square in half and unfold.

2
Fold and unfold again.

3a & b
Turn the paper over.

4
Fold and unfold diagonally.

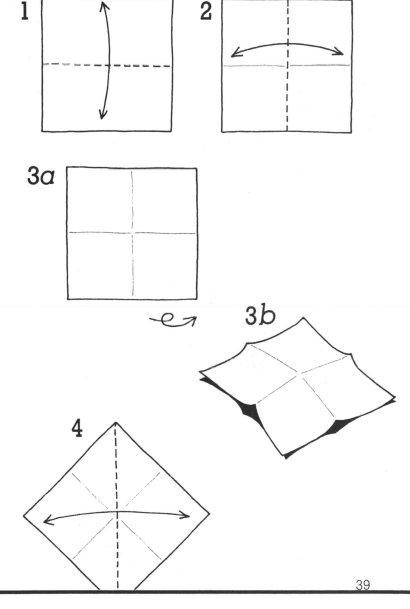

continued...

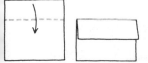
valley fold

mountain fold

existing crease

X-ray view

unfold

5

And again fold diagonally.

6

Hold the outside points and push them downwards.

7

The centre will come together like this.

8

Flatten so that there are two points on each side.

9

Swing the top left point up.

10

Push down to open out the point.

11

Centre and flatten out the point.

12

Fold behind where indicated.

13

Open out the folds.

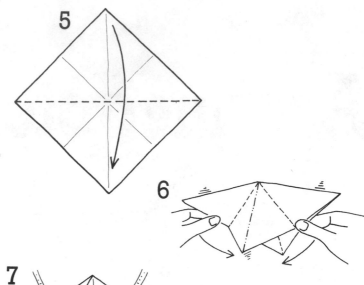

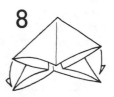

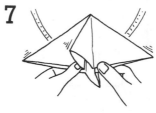

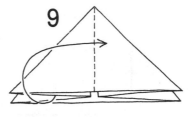

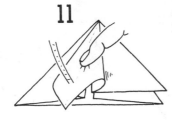

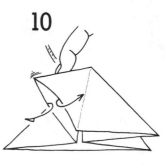

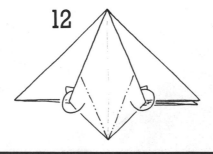

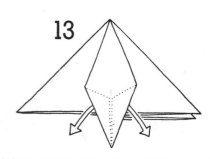

←—→	*fold and unfold*	℮↗ *turn over*	○ *hold here*
•→•	*fold one dot onto the other*	—→ *fold to the front*	⟋○ *pull*
— —✂	*cut*	—⌐ *fold behind*	► *push here*

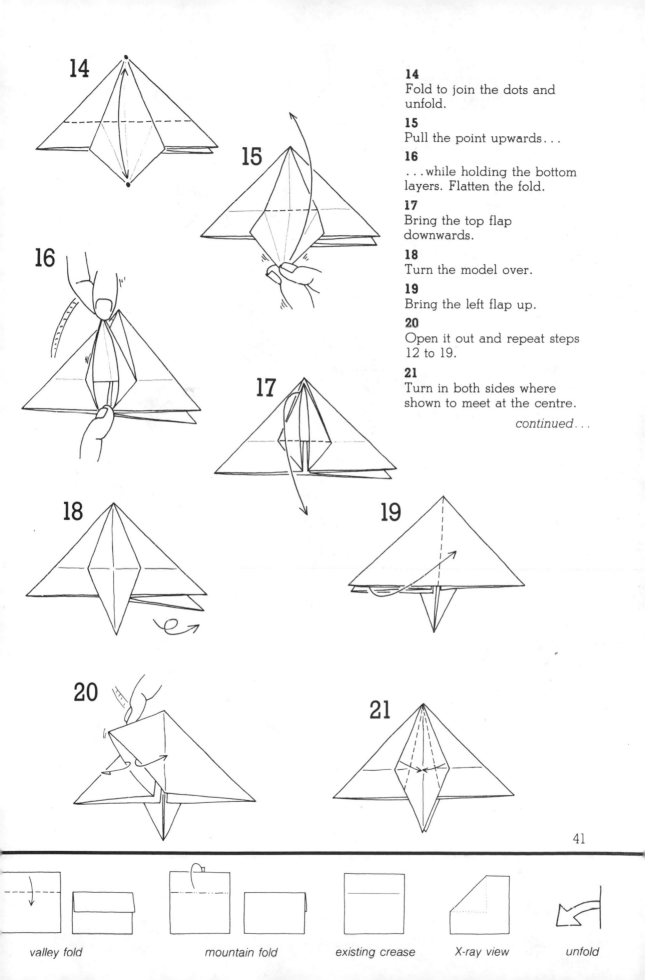

14
Fold to join the dots and unfold.

15
Pull the point upwards...

16
...while holding the bottom layers. Flatten the fold.

17
Bring the top flap downwards.

18
Turn the model over.

19
Bring the left flap up.

20
Open it out and repeat steps 12 to 19.

21
Turn in both sides where shown to meet at the centre.

continued...

41

valley fold   mountain fold   existing crease   X-ray view   unfold

22
Bring the top point to meet the bottom point.

23
The point behind will unfold automatically. Pull it right up and flatten it.

24
Fold and unfold where shown.

25
Fold where indicated tucking fingers under the flaps and bringing them towards the centre while pushing where shown.

26
Fold the model in half.

27
Inside reverse fold the left side, the neck section, and fold back the outer layer at the right. This will form the legs.

28
Inside reverse fold the neck to create the head. Fold and unfold the wing tips at the top. Fold down the wings where shown. Cut down the centre of the leg section to make two legs and outside reverse fold the tail section.

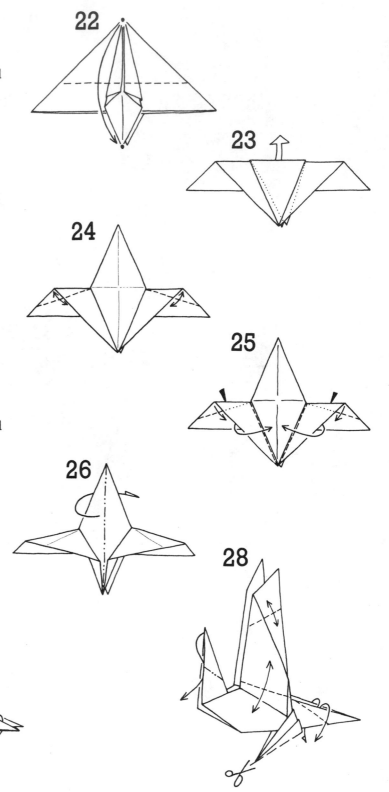

 fold and unfold

 fold one dot onto the other

cut

turn over

fold to the front

fold behind

hold here

 pull

push here

29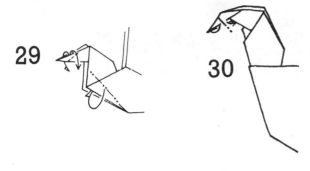

30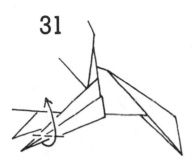

29
Crease and outside reverse fold the nose and fold to streamline the creature's chest area.

30
Tuck in the nose point.

31
At the end of each leg, fold to make a foot.

32
The completed Archaeopteryx. Now you can pose the question of which came first, the Archaeopteryx or the egg?

31

32

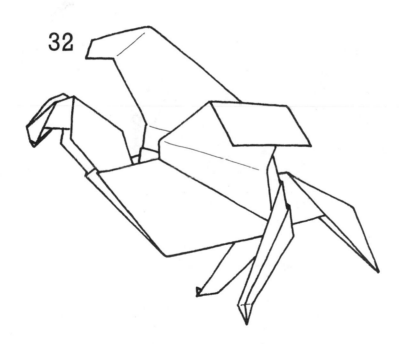

valley fold

mountain fold

existing crease

X-ray view

unfold

Brachiosaurus

This is another sauropod like the Brontosaurus, but much heavier. The Brachiosaurus is considered to be one of the largest and heaviest of dinosaurs, weighing more than eighty tonnes (eighty tons)! They lived during the upper Jurassic period and could stand as tall as fifteen metres (fifty feet). If they were still alive today they'd certainly clean up your local grocer's shop in a single meal!

1
Make up to step 15 of the Triceratops (pages 34, 35 and 36) but omit step 11. Turn the model over.

2
Fold in on each side to make the neck narrower. Inside reverse fold the legs to make feet.

3
Fold back the rump sections on either side. Another inside reverse fold on each side swings the feet to the front again.

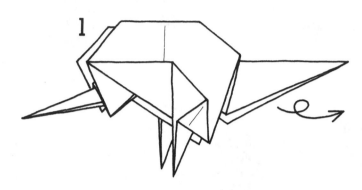

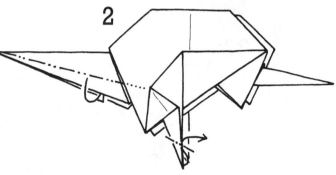

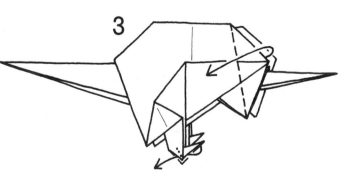

⟵⟶	fold and unfold	⟲→	turn over	O	hold here
•⟶•	fold one dot onto the other	⟶	fold to the front	⟍°O	pull
— ⋅— ✂	cut	⟶	fold behind	►	push here

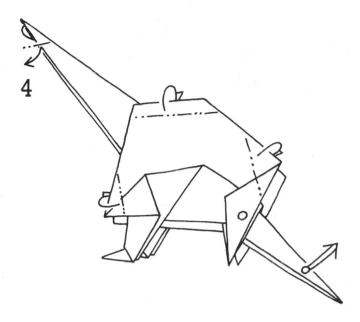

4

Inside reverse fold the small head, and shape the body by folding corners as marked in towards the centre on both sides. Finally hold the creature firmly. Pull up the tail and curl it...

5

...and you have a completed Brachiosaurus to grace your vegetable garden or tossed salad.

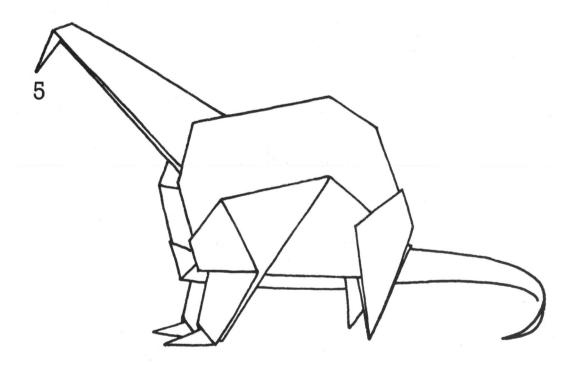

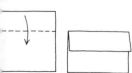
valley fold

mountain fold

existing crease

X-ray view

unfold

Corythosaurus

The Corythosaurus is an unusual creature which features a "helmet" covering its skull. No one knows the purpose of the helmet; perhaps it assisted the brain to function better! If you like head-banging music, your Corythosaurus will certainly cope with it!

The Corythosaurus belongs to the crested duckbill group which is part of the ornithopod group of dinosaurs. These herbivorous bipeds lived during the late Cretaceous period around ninety million years ago.

1
Begin by making up to step 17 of Dimetrodon (pages 15 16 and 17), then mountain fold the top sides behind.

2
Crease, then inside reverse fold the inside peaks as shown, eventually to form legs.

3
This crease pattern indicates rabbit ears. (See page 5 for a refresher if needed.)

4
Make the rabbit ear as shown. Repeat on the left side and flatten both sides.

5
Fold the model in half.

⟵⟶	fold and unfold	ℓ↗	turn over	O	hold here	
•⟶•	fold one dot onto the other	⟶	fold to the front		pull	
--✂	cut	⟿	fold behind	▶	push here	

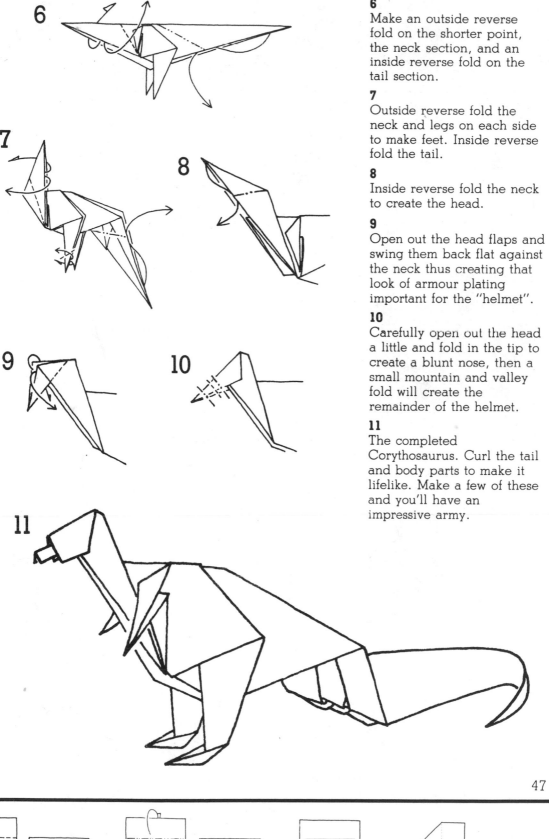

6
Make an outside reverse fold on the shorter point, the neck section, and an inside reverse fold on the tail section.

7
Outside reverse fold the neck and legs on each side to make feet. Inside reverse fold the tail.

8
Inside reverse fold the neck to create the head.

9
Open out the head flaps and swing them back flat against the neck thus creating that look of armour plating important for the "helmet".

10
Carefully open out the head a little and fold in the tip to create a blunt nose, then a small mountain and valley fold will create the remainder of the helmet.

11
The completed Corythosaurus. Curl the tail and body parts to make it lifelike. Make a few of these and you'll have an impressive army.

valley fold	*mountain fold*	*existing crease*	*X-ray view*	*unfold*

Campbell Morris is a graphic artist and origami expert. He lives in Australia.

The Dinosaur Club

This is an exclusive club for the elite of paper palaeontologists who desire only the best in paper craftsmanship. Actually, there are clubs that handle not only "dinosaurs" but general origami. If you are a paper enthusiast I suggest you contact these people:

Clare Chamberlain
Origami Australia
31/2 Goderich Street
Perth WA 6000

David Brill
British Origami Society
12 Thorn Road
Bramhall, Stockport
SK7 1HQ
United Kingdom

Friends of the Origami Centre of America
15 West 77th Street
New York, NY 10024

Origami Centre of America
31 Union Square West
New York, NY 10003

West Coast Origami Guild
PO Box 90601
Pasadena, CA 91109